The Atlas of
Famous Battles
of the American
Revolution ™

The Battle of Monmouth

Scott P. Waldman

The Rosen Publishing Group's
PowerKids Press ™
New York

Published in 2003 by The Rosen Publishing Group, Inc.
29 East 21st Street, New York, NY 10010

First Edition

Editor: Nancy MacDonell Smith

Book Design: Michael J. Caroleo

Photo Credits: Cover, title page, pp. 12, 15, 16,19 (maps) Maria Melendez; cover, title page, p. 7 (Washington) © Geoffrey Clements/CORBIS; cover, title page, pp. 4 (bottom) 8 (Clinton), 16 (cannon) © Bettmann CORBIS; p. 4 (map) Michael Dong; pp. 4 (bayonet), 12 (sword), 19 (rifle) courtesy of the George C. Neumann Collection, Valley Forge National Historic Park, photos by Cindy Reiman; pp. 7 (bottom), 8 (bottom) 11 (bottom, inset right), 12 (bottom), 16 (bottom, insets) Dover Pictorial Archive Series; pp. 7 (inset top), 15 (inset bottom right) ©CORBIS; pp. 7 (map), 8 (map), 11 (map), 20 (map) Map Division, Library of Congress.

Waldman, Scott P.
The Battle of Monmouth / Scott P. Waldman.— 1st ed.
     p. cm. — (The atlas of famous battles of the American Revolution)
Includes bibliographical references and index.
Summary: Details the advancements of the British and American troops at the Battle of Monmouth in New Jersey in 1778.
  ISBN 0-8239-6330-6
1. Monmouth, Battle of, 1778—Juvenile literature. [1. Monmouth, Battle of, 1778. 2. United States—History—Revolution, 1775–1783—Campaigns.] I. Title. II. Series.
  E241.M7 W34 2003
  973.3'34—dc21

                                                                                            2001007777

Manufactured in the United States of America

Contents

N

Schuylkill River

Washington's Headquarters

to Philadelphia

The Lonely Winter

The Americans surrendered New York City to the British in 1776, but they continued to increase their strength. General George Washington and 10,000 of his **Continental army** soldiers spent the winter of 1777–1778 at Valley Forge, Pennsylvania. The winter was cold and difficult for the men, but they worked hard at becoming better soldiers. The colonists were trained by European **officers** to fight like the British soldiers, who were known as **regulars**. The colonists were taught how to march as a group and how to use a **bayonet**. In May 1778, France signed a **treaty** that recognized American independence from Britain. France and England were enemies. The French decided to help the colonists fight the British. The French sent men and supplies to the colonies. The French support worried the British generals. With the help of the French, the colonists were ready to rid America of the British.

General Washington and his troops camped at Valley Forge, Pennsylvania, during the winter of 1777–1778. Valley Forge is on the Schuylkill River, about 25 miles (40 km) from Philadelphia. **Bottom:** General Washington suffered through the cold winter along with his men. About 2,500 American soldiers died at Valley Forge because of the cold and the lack of food.

The Two Sides Fight

The British controlled Philadelphia in the cold winter of 1778–1779. By the spring, they had almost run out of food. The regulars began to look for food in the countryside around Philadelphia. General Washington heard about this. He knew that if he cut off the regulars' food supply, they would be weakened. On May 18, 1778, Washington sent 2,000 men led by Major General Marquis de Lafayette, a Frenchman who was helping the colonists, to Barren Hill near Philadelphia. The British attacked Lafayette early on May 20, 1778. The regulars knew that if they **defeated** Lafayette and his men, it would be very difficult for the Continental army to recover. Lafayette and his men fought hard. This surprised the regulars. They stopped their attack for a moment because they were worried that Lafayette might have more men than they had originally thought. Lafayette and his men used this brief break to **retreat** to safety.

General Washington chose Barren Hill as the best place to attack the British. **Bottom:** *Before sending them to Barren Hill with General Lafayette, General Washington encouraged his cold and hungry troops.* **Top Right:** *General Lafayette was trusted and well liked by General Washington. Washington thought of the younger man as a son.*

SCALE

0   0.5   1 Mile   2 Miles

0   0.5   1   1.5 Km

COLOR KEY

Colonial Militia:

British Regulars:

Barren Hill

General George Washington

COLOR KEY
Colonial Militia:
British Regulars:

to New York

Philadelphia

General Sir Henry Clinton

The British retreated on foot or horseback, carrying their belongings with them.

The British Leave Town

The British became worried when they could not win the battle against Lafayette. General Sir Henry Clinton, a high-ranking British officer who had fought in many battles, wanted to leave Philadelphia. General Clinton decided to march his entire army to New York City, which was more than 100 miles (161 km) away. He thought his troops would be in a better position to fight the colonists there because there were so many British soldiers in New York. It would have been safer to travel by sea, but General Clinton had to take 3,000 horses with him and he didn't have enough ships for them. The regulars had to travel on foot. On June 18, 1778, Clinton left for New York with all 10,000 of the regulars who had been staying in and around Philadelphia. As soon as the British left, General Washington and his army of 10,000 colonists took over Philadelphia. General Washington held a meeting with other colonial leaders to decide what to do next. They decided to chase the regulars.

◀ *The colonists chased the regulars from Philadelphia to New York. General Washington decided that the colonists' winter training had made them strong enough to fight the British in New York.*

Preparing for Battle

The regulars had already been marching toward New York City for a few days when the colonists left Philadelphia to chase them. It took almost a week for the colonists to catch up to the regulars. On June 26, 1778, Washington decided to attack the **rear guard** of the British army. The regulars had stopped for a rest at the **courthouse** in the town of Monmouth, New Jersey. That same day, General Washington ordered 5,000 troops to get ready for battle. That night the colonists camped a few miles (km) from the courthouse. On June 27, 1778, they got into position for an attack on the courthouse where the British were resting. The attack was planned for the next day. At 4:00 A.M. on June 28, 1778, the regulars started moving the first part of their army toward New York. By 7:00 A.M. half of the colonial force was moving toward the courthouse to get into position to attack the regular rear guard. At 8:00 A.M. the regular rear guard began to leave Monmouth courthouse.

The Continental army followed the British through New Jersey to the town of Monmouth. The British were headed for New York City but stopped to rest in Monmouth. When he saw that the British had stopped, General Washington decided to attack.

COLOR KEY

Colonial Militia:
British Regulars:

to New York

Monmouth courthouse

Monmouth

Philadelphia

The British stopped to rest at the Monmouth courthouse.

Instead of attacking the British right away, the Americans spent two nights camped near the courthouse before carrying out their plan.

West Ravine

Courthouse

Though eighteenth-century soldiers used guns and cannons, swords were used in hand-to-hand fighting. Officers carried fancier swords than did ordinary soldiers.

N

The Battle Begins

The regular rear guard stayed behind to keep the colonists from attacking the rest of the troops. At 10:00 A.M. the colonists attacked the rear guard. The colonists thought that they could defeat the regulars easily. The colonists didn't realize how many men were in the rear guard. The regulars quickly started to surround the colonists. The colonists were **startled** by this sudden move. They realized that they were outnumbered by the regulars. The colonists were ordered to retreat. The attack surprised the colonists because it had gone differently from what they had planned. They moved back 3 miles (5 km) to West Ravine, New Jersey, where Washington and his large army were waiting. The regulars continued to advance on Washington's army. General Washington was angry that his men had run away. He **organized** them to fight again.

The rear guard was larger than the colonists realized. The battle turned out to be more difficult than the colonists had expected. **Bottom:** *General Washington was not pleased with his troops' retreat. He ordered them to prepare themselves for battle once again.*

Washington to the Rescue

Washington got his men into position at West Ravine so that they could **defend** themselves. The regulars did not know that they were about to go into battle with the entire Continental army. They continued to chase the colonists that they could see. When General Clinton realized that he was about to fight General Washington's entire army, Clinton sent for more soldiers from the group that was moving toward New York. This gave the colonists time to get themselves ready for the battle. The colonists took cannons to the top of Comb's Hill, which was nearby. They knew it would be easier to fire on the regulars from a high point. From the top of the hill, the colonists could see the entire British army. The regulars could not get up the hill very easily with their heavy packs. By 12:00 P.M. on June 28, 1778, it had become very hot. Both the colonists and the regulars were wearing very heavy cotton uniforms. Men on both sides were **exhausted** by the heat of the sun. Many of them died because of it.

Inset left: Along with having to wear their heavy cotton uniforms, the troops had to carry all their supplies with them. **Inset right:** *Molly Pitcher was one of the heroes of the Battle of Monmouth. She was bringing water to the hot and thirsty troops when her husband, a gunner, was injured. Molly stepped in and took his place until reinforcements arrived.*

General Washington gathered his men at the top of Comb's Hill. The British approached from the east.

West Ravine

to New York

Comb's Hill

Courthouse

N

Comb's Hill

West Ravine

Both sides used cannons during the battle. This cannon can be seen today at Valley Forge.

N

COLOR KEY

Colonial Militia:

British Regulars:

A Break from the Fighting

Both sides fought very hard. The colonists fought bravely, but once again the regulars forced them back. More men died or were injured in the early afternoon of June 28, 1778, than at any other part of the day. The regulars appeared to be winning until General Washington stepped in with fresh troops. The fresh troops went to the **front line**. The men who had been fighting so hard against the regulars were allowed to rest. More cannons were set up nearby. The colonists fired the cannons on the regulars. Many regulars were killed. They could no longer advance on the colonists. The colonists took back the ground that they had lost. The regulars made two more attempts to force back the colonists. They were stopped by the cannons. There was a brief break in the battle while the officers on both sides figured out what their next move would be. The men used the break in the battle to take a much-needed rest.

◀ *The regulars forced the Continental army back several times that day.* **Bottom:** *General Washington first sent about half his troops to Monmouth. Later he arrived with fresh men.* **Inset Left:** *The men used the break in the battle to cool off with water. The weather was very hot that day.* **Inset Top:** *George Washington had his men bring up more cannons for their fight against the British.*

The End of a Long Fight

The colonists used the break in the fighting to get rid of their heavy coats. In the meantime, the regulars formed into a tight **unit**. They marched toward the colonists. Then they **charged** the colonists. The colonists waited until the regulars got close before firing. The officer leading the regular charge was killed. This made the regulars very angry. They charged at the colonists again. Neither side wanted to give up. The colonists used the skills they had been taught at Valley Forge. Men on both sides quickly became too tired to continue. Neither side was winning. General Washington and General Clinton each ordered their men to pull back. By 8:30 P.M. the battle had ended. As the sun set, both sides made camp for the night.

By the end of that very hot day, both armies were exhausted and ready to retreat to their camps.
Bottom: *The Battle of Monmouth was fought in a small area. Soldiers often came face-to-face with the enemy during the long day of fighting. This was the longest battle of the American Revolution.*

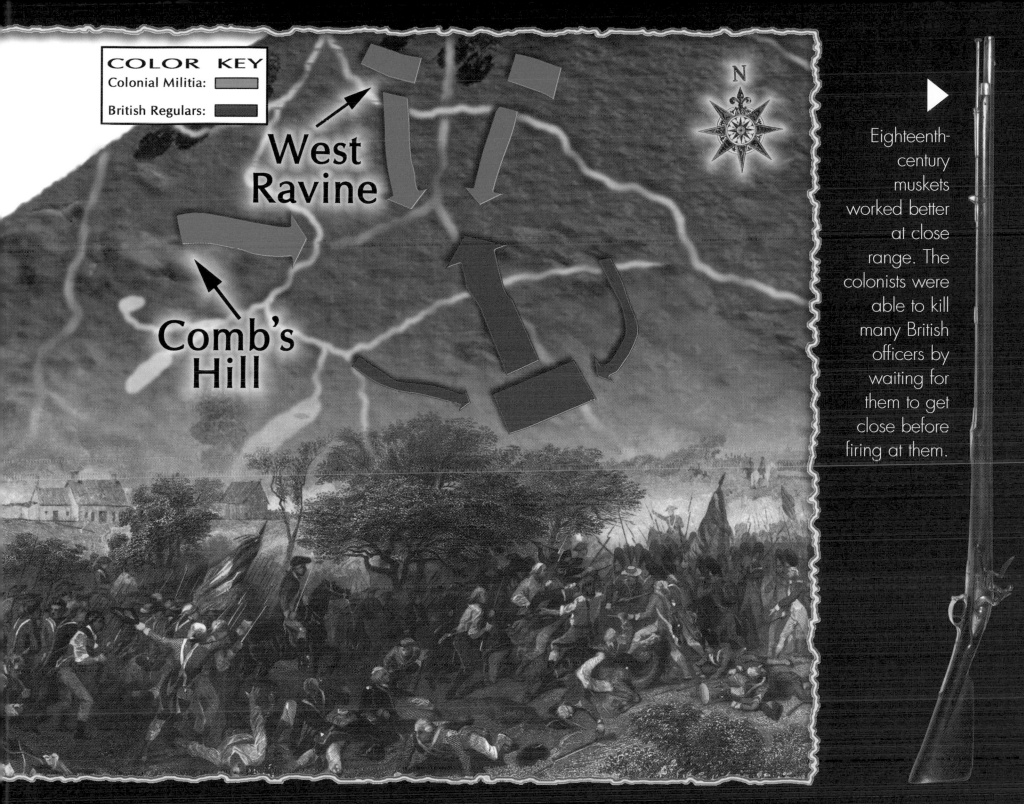

COLOR KEY
Colonial Militia:
British Regulars:

West Ravine

Comb's Hill

N

Eighteenth-century muskets worked better at close range. The colonists were able to kill many British officers by waiting for them to get close before firing at them.

New York City

Sandy Point

Monmouth

The colonists proved that they could fight as a united force at the Battle of Monmouth.

COLOR KEY

Colonial Militia:

British Regulars:

The Regulars Disappear

General Washington prepared his men to attack at dawn. However, the British did not want to continue the battle. General Clinton ordered his men to get ready to leave in the middle of the night. They quietly packed up their camp and left in the dark so that they would not be seen. The regulars were so quiet that the colonists didn't realize they were gone until the next morning. The Battle of Monmouth had ended. It was the biggest one-day battle in the American Revolution. Neither side had beaten the other. The colonists had been able to attack and to hold out against the British army. The regulars had been able to get their supplies to Sandy Point, New Jersey, and then to New York City. Both sides had lost many men, a large number of them from heat exhaustion.

◄ General Clinton and his troops retreated to New York during the night. General Washington had expected to continue the battle in the morning. **Inset:** Each army lost about 350 soldiers.

The War Continues

Though the Battle of Monmouth ended with the British retreat, many colonists still were not convinced that independence from England was a good idea. They were worried that the colonists were fighting a war they could not win. However, the Battle of Monmouth proved that the Continental army was powerful enough to fight the British army. The winter training at Valley Forge had made the colonists better soldiers.

Monmouth was also the last major battle of the war to be fought in the northern colonies. For the next few years neither side had an advantage over the other. The war was hard on both sides. Most people just wanted it to be finished. The British marched south, where they tried to win support. The colonists fought hard to get the regulars out of the South. This led to the Battle of Yorktown in Virginia in 1781, which was the last major battle of the American Revolution.

Glossary

bayonet (BAY-oh-net) A knife attached to the front end of a rifle.

charged (CHARJD) Made a rushed attack.

Continental army (kon-tin-EN-tul AR-mee) The army of patriots created in 1775, with George Washington as its commander in chief.

courthouse (KORT-hows) A place where trials are held.

defeated (dih-FEET-ed) Made someone lose.

defend (dih-FEND) To protect from harm.

exhausted (eg-ZAW-sted) Very tired.

front line (FRUNT LYN) The troops at the front of a battle.

officers (AH-fuh-surz) People who command other people in the armed forces.

organized (OR-guh-nyzd) To have things neat and in order.

rear guard (REER GARD) The soldiers who protect the back of an army.

regulars (REH-gyuh-lurz) Professional British soldiers.

retreat (ree-TREET) To back away from a fight.

startled (STAR-tuld) Surprised.

treaty (TREE-tee) A formal agreement, signed and agreed upon by each party.

unit (YOO-nit) A group of soldiers.

Index

Primary Sources

Page 4. *English Long-Land Pattern Bayonet.* Steel, c. 1770s. Valley Forge National Historic Park. This bayonet was meant to be used with the Long-Land Pattern Musket. This musket was 4 inches (10 cm) longer than the Short-Land Pattern Musket. British and American soldiers used both types of guns during the American Revolution. Bayonets were an important part of combat because guns took so long to reload. Once they fired their muskets, soldiers would often have to fight face-to-face. This type of bayonet was shaped like a triangle. It made a bigger, more serious wound than did a bayonet with a straight blade. Early in the war, the colonists had very few bayonets. The French supplied the Continental army with bayonets later in the war. **Page 7.** *Plan de la retraite de Barren Hill en Pensilvanie (Map of the Retreat From Barren Hill in Pennsylvania).* Capitaine Michel de Chesnoy. Ink, watercolor, wash, and lead pencil on paper mounted on cloth, 1778. The Map Division of the Library of Congress. This map was drawn by Captain Chesnoy, General Lafayette's aide-de-camp, or assistant officer. Chesnoy was one of the most skilled mapmakers of his time. He made several very beautiful maps for Lafayette during the American Revolution. Six of these maps were recently bought by the Library of Congress. They are a valuable addition to our knowledge of the battles of the American Revolution. **Page 12.** *Cavalry Sword.* Steel, c. 1770s. Valley Forge National Historic Park. This type of sword was meant to be used by a soldier riding a horse. Since most ordinary soldiers couldn't afford to have horses, this sword probably belonged to an officer. It is part of a collection of weapons at Valley Forge National Historic Park. In 1893, Valley Forge was made a state park. In 1977, Valley Forge became a National Historic Park. This was done so that people will always remember what happened there. **Page 16.** *Cannon.* Iron and wood, c. 1775–81. Valley Forge National Historic Park. Cannons were an important part of eighteenth-century warfare. If an army without a cannon had to fight an enemy that did have a cannon, the army without the cannon would almost always lose the battle. Large cannons had wheels so they could be moved. Smaller cannons, which were called grasshoppers, had iron legs. **Page 19.** *Short-Land Pattern Musket.* Brass, wood, and iron, c. 1775–81. Valley Forge National Historic Park. This type of gun had been used by the British army since 1718. It was often called the Brown Bess. Loading and firing a musket took several steps. Before a battle, a soldier would fold small pieces of paper around the lead bullet and a little bit of gunpowder. This was a paper cartridge. To get the gun ready to fire, the soldier would first bite off the top of the cartridge. Then he would shake a little of the gunpowder into a part of the gun called the priming pan. This gunpowder would help to create the explosion that pushed the bullet out of the barrel. Then he would put the cartridge into the barrel of the gun. Next he took out his ramrod, then inserted that into the barrel of the musket and pounded down the cartridge. Then he put the ramrod back into its holder underneath the barrel of the gun. Finally, the gun was ready to be fired. It was hard to know where the bullet would go after it left the gun. It was very hard for a soldier to hit a target that was more than 50 feet (15 m) away.

Web Sites

Due to the changing nature of Internet links, PowerKids Press has developed an online list of Web sites related to the subject of this book. This site is updated regularly. Please use this link to access the list:

www.powerkidslinks.com/afbar/monmouth/